Analysis of Market and Product Mixes using Ryan-air's

Ryan-air are currently sitting as the biggest "No Frills" Airline in Europe. They have grown from a single plane company to where they are currently through offering the customer what was needed during times of financial hardship affordable air travel.

Ryan-air currently offers a number of different tangible and intangible products and services, with new initiatives been added, and starting their "life cycle". Although as a company they offer many services, it could still be said the variation shows little product mix length. The reason for this being that the services offered are all in one market.

As you will see below, the services and product all tie in with each other showing good width of product mix. This gives the opportunity for customers to pick and choose which products they want and need, or purchasing all these products together forms a package, which could be seen as the ultimate package Ryan-air has to offer. Below is a list of current services/ products, I shall group them in relation to where the lay within their life cycle using a variation of the "Boston Matrix".

STARS	QUESTION MARK
-> Low cost travel -> Regular point to point flights across Europe -> 100% safety record -> Fewer lots bags and cancelled flights -> Secondary airports	->Technological fast check in -> More focused customer service -> Family deal -> Flights during non peak/ unsociable hours
CASH COWS	DOGS
Commission based ancillary incomes, such as; -> Hertz car hire -> Various hotels -> Phone cards -> Bus tickets	-> Providing controversy to generate free publicity -> Their low airtime winter position

STARS:- classed as stars, these services are are most profitable, these are mid life cycle, and They offer excellent perceived and actual value. They hold a high market share and generate large revenues

QUESTION MARKS:- classed as questionable as there are relatively new services, with time could grow into stars. they hold a low market share but providing high growth

CASH COWS:-these provide steady but relatively low revenue the. they have reached maturity and hold a high market share, these don't generally need much of a outlay

DOGS: these may be heading towards the end of the life cycle and now generate little revenue or hold a significant market share. A closer look into these services is need to determine whether to discontinue or spend some capital regenerating the service.

LIFE CYCLE

The life cycle of a products is resource that highlights which products/services are profitable, which are a steady source of of revenue, and which are in need of regeneration or need to be discontinued. It uses the Market share held and the growth in profit as a guide, and shows how old a service or product are. See a example below

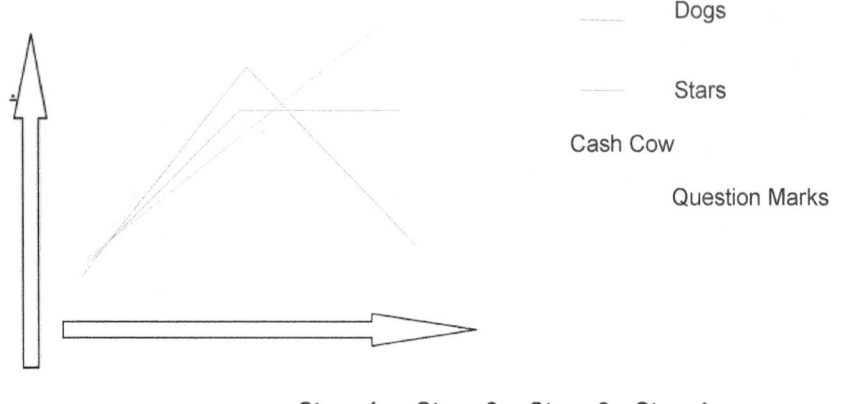

                                                          Dogs

                                                          Stars

                                              Cash Cow

                                              Question Marks

Stage 1.   Stage 2.   Stage 3   Stage4
Introduction.   Growth   Maturity.   Decline

As you can see from the graph its shows the stage of the life cycle relating to the products usefulness regarding profit. The QUESTION MARKS show products In stage one of there life. These need more time to grow and mature and need funds spent on promoting and grabbing peoples attention.

The STARS have grown and continue to do so into maturity whilst being the source of a large percentage of income. Similar to the CASH COWS except these are not growing a any considerable rate, yet they provide a steady stream of income, there stabilized in there market.

The DOGS are the services that have had there day but are becoming obsolete, due to things such as a change in behaviour or competition. One way to deal with these is to stop the particular service or product, making funds and hours available for new initiatives. Another would be to regenerate, this would mean using finances to re-promote after applying necessary changes other forms of re-invention may include; package redesign, added/extra features, drop in price to fend off competitors and encourage custom, re-marketed in to another segment with weaker competition.

There are pro's and con's to Ryan-air's Product mix and strategy. It could be said that there is not enough activity in different segments of the market, therefore they are missing potential opportunity's regarding growth and building there brand name in other markets. Offering more services equals more profit? Not always because if you look at the pro's of this approach then you could say, they can apply more focus and personnel to this segment having a higher chance of succeeds. You may also argue that they spend less finances as there are not marketing products, in several segments, trying to target differing customers. Ryan-air's decision to concentrate on budget travel has seen a massive success, and other company's try to emulate this strategy, or diversify into this segment. This is even though " No Frills" seems to go against perception of a "Quality Brand".

DELIVERY AND DISTRIBUTION

Ryan-air's distribution and the delivery of its services is a major influence on how they set prices as low as they do, and in turn offer excellent perceived value. The purchaser, after experiencing the service is then entitled to judge the actual value provided. The practice of offering a kind of after service is a useful tool in regards to retaining their custom. After service is a segment of the market in which Ryan-air could look to improve and develop.

Ryan-air's aims to offer the cheapest ticket prices in Europe, to achieve their objective, they have cut back on a lot of added extras, such as in flight meals, boarding tunnels etc. As well as this the way in which they distribute their service is a massive boost to their cost cutting methods. The ways in which they cut cost at this stage of the campaign is by again stripping back and doing a lot of the process in house. For example they;

---> cut out travel agents, reaching the customer directly through the Internet, through its informative website and clever publicity
---> Save money on customer facing staff and staff training. Customers book online, and there is no check in desks etc
---> Offer other company's advertising opportunity's through branding on there fleet etc
---> Up sell other company's services/products generating income through commissions

These cost cutting measurements concerning distribution methods not only returns healthy margins for Ryan-air but also provides convenience to the customer. With their being no travel agent to deal and booking online, customers can browse at leisure without pressure. The can book 24/7 using the website to purchase single items such as flights, or they can build the whole travel package, tailoring it to meet there own needs.

Tangible delivery; in regards to on time flights, luggage security and fast check in are delivered through various methods.

-->Allowing less hold luggage, this saves time on loading, means planes are lighter saving fuel, and cost
-->Faster turnaround of fleet, meaning more flights, more generated income and happy customers
-->Rejecting check in desks and opting for ticket scan, means again faster turnarounds on flights
-->A focus on baggage handlers resulting in fewer lost luggage, less customer complaints and more return buyers

All this contributes to Ryan-air amassing large numbers of passengers per year, This is also good business for the airports themselves. So much so that they have become a source of revenue, as they are willing to pay Ryan-air to use there Airports, as they bring custom from across the UK and Europe through their doors.

PRICE SETTING

Ryan-air's strategy when setting there prices is simple. Offer the lowest price short/mid haul flights in Europe. This is an objective they have met through previously mentioned cost saving methods, thus passing the reductions onto customers. As well as these cost reducing methods however, there are other avenues of saving to be covered

--> Purchasing methods. They have in the past used the strategy of purchasing fleet when other airlines won't, for example after 9/11. Manufacturers can't simply abort a process mid-build, meaning aircraft that no one wants. Step up Ryan-air, who purchase these planes, and strike up further future deals at knocked down prices.
--> They operate One single type of plane, by doing this they reduce maintenance costs This also when added to the number of planes they run aids in more flights, as planes spend less time grounded, and more time generating income.

--> Bulk purchase and good Business to Business communication leads to reduced fuel costs, meaning more flights, more savings and more revenue. This method also may counter act any fluctuation in fuel costs.

EXTERNAL AND INTERNAL INFLUENCES

Pricing strategy's take into account many factors which can be controlled and measured, like the various cost cutting strategy's. There are other possible factors Externally that are, it could be said "out of there hands". However its important to factor these in to a strategy if only to be prepared to adapt the service or price offered. There are Six possible external influences on the airline industry, and can be demonstrated using the PESTLE model.

Political- the airline industry is tightly restricted and monitored on issues such as competition and sector monopoly, international trading and air and duty tax. These cant be directly effected but must be prepared for regarding extra finances.

Economic- Here a healthy economy is a added bonus for most airlines, look at Ryan-air's past figures, these indicate that as a brand, they thrive in economic difficulties. Its down to disposable income, which in turn is influenced by, industry, production and manufacturing, levels of import /export and the changing prices in the oil sector.

Social- Largely down to customer behaviour which is very unpredictable at times but can be influenced partially by looking at factors such social class, advocacy, different cultures, cultural attitudes, values and beliefs and your public perception.

Technological- The use of the internet as a buying tool has helped Ryan-air with cost cutting and reaching more potential customers, it also poses the threat of competition With more information readily available customers are able to seek out the best perceived value. It also aides the competition with pricing strategy's and offering improvements on Ryan-air's Social media can spread bad feedback internationally

Legal- This ties in with the political issues, such as, time restrictions, different laws in different destinations, international trade laws, employment laws regarding employees in different countries etc

Environmental- Here Aviation company's see pressure coming from pressure groups, political and government agencies as well as the public. Environmental issues have become more common place, and generally making people more aware and conscious. To be seen as "Environmentally Friendly" is important for CRM and again have they may hold a modicum of control over some aspects of their perception

Internal factors:- pertaining to cost, positioning, market and product mix are factors you are able to control mostly. These can be recorded for analysis using the SWOT model. I've varied it slightly in layout only.

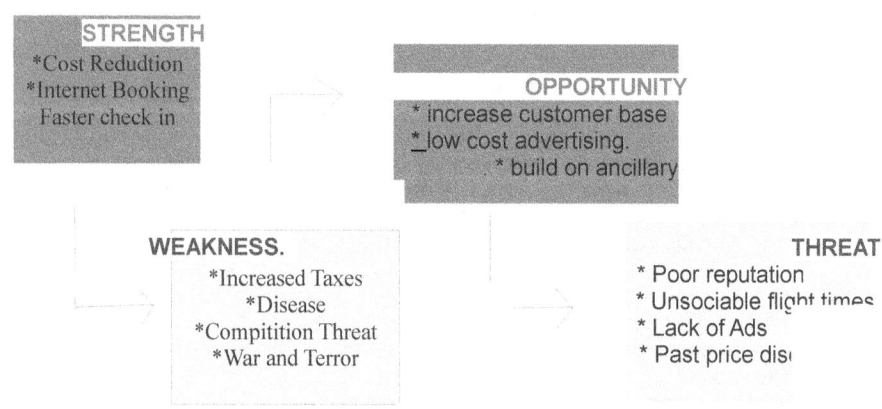

STRENGTH
*Cost Redudtion
*Internet Booking
Faster check in

OPPORTUNITY
* increase customer base
* low cost advertising.
* build on ancillary

WEAKNESS.
*Increased Taxes
*Disease
*Compitition Threat
*War and Terror

THREAT
* Poor reputation
* Unsociable flight times
* Lack of Ads
* Past price dis

This should provide researchable information regarding strategy, time band revenue needed, price strategy and together with PESTLE an idea as to whether are segment could reap profit cost effectively and level of competition. It could be said us a constant reminder and should be completed regularly in order to adapt with any market changes, and to adopt a emergency plan for uncontrollable circumstances.

PROMOITIONS

Ryan-air's currant emotional activity has seen a raid growth in the market share, and their spend little approach has been a success To change a successful model I believe would be a mistake, however if we are to follow customer behaviour they must be able to adapt it.

The promotional strategy for the following Six months below is following on from the cost effective model used with maybe a slight increase in spend in order to really grab the attention of the public. The objective is to increase the winter flights and in turn increase our share in this segment. This is a new initiative, hence the for mentioned slight increase in spending. The first step is the Wow factor, to gain the interest of the trend setters, the innovators or "Early Adopters". If we are to achieve this with a clear defined message, offer value and excellent service, its these people that will advertise for Ryan-air, through advocacy, word of mouth, and of course social media. The costs then decrease to where Ryan-air are comfortable as the message spreads on to the 'Early and Late majority's", who between them could account for up to 70-80% of future sales. To show the Adoption process of a services please find a basic model below.

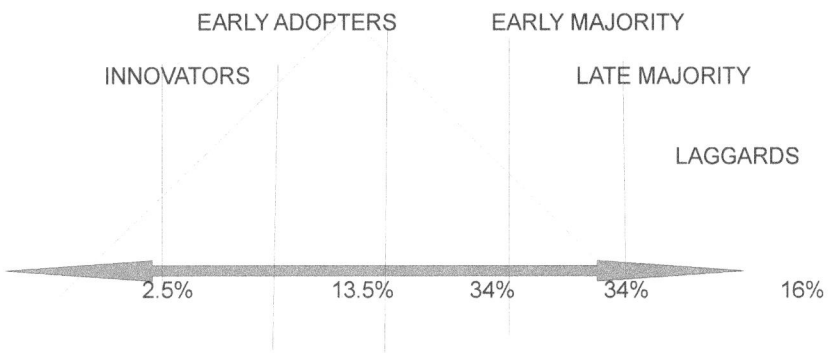

As yo can see attracting the early adopters and innovators is the start to gaining the steady and profitable majority groups. As the life span goes on into the laggard section it is possible you may need extra promotion, price drops etc. This section is where moire investment of hours and finance may be required.

I believe the evolution of the marketing process benefit's Ryan-air's strategy of keeping cost at a minimum. The introduction of the internet means advertising costs have reduced, its even possible to benefit from free advertising through social media etc. I propose that Ryan-air run a promotion leading up to the Baron winter months, offering winter sun at a discount. The use of social media as a advertising tool would mean little costs, they would need to cover the discounted cost of the holidays, but if there was a requirement of the selected person having to share this promotion then the advert becomes multi-national very quickly and very cheaply.

April	May	June	July	August	September
Direct	Facebook	Facebook	Direct	Facebook	Facebook
*Emails *Inboxes *Letters, *Surveys to find Customers Wants *Explain compitition	*Professional Facebook page *Chance to win Prizes for sharing The page	*up campaign Offering More incentive To share the Page EG free luggage etc	*Direct marketing To businesses Offering discount Winter travel For exclusivity (loyalty scheme)	*More focus on Brand advocacy Extending loyalty Scheme to non Business passengers	* last chance to Enter comp. Entice the laggards

This I believe is a risk free relatively cost effective market strategy with the potential of the Ryan-air brand reaching mass numbers very quickly. Initial outlay of man power, cost of holidays and other prizes should be worth it if we can attracted more potential customers. Direct mail and manpower being the other main objective to increase winter flights for Ryan-air but in a cost effective way to generate profit and increased market share.
The success of a new initiative is dependent on many factors. Before the development and launching stage, Ryan-air needs to research the market it intends to target. The 4 P's of marketing mix are the variable factors which a company has some control over, these are Price, Product, Promotion and Place.(McCarthy)

PRODUCT	PRICE	PROMOTION	PLACE
*Desirability *How will it be used *How much will it cost *Does it fit with the brand *Any after-care offered *How to package the product/service * How convenient is it to purchase	*Cost of development *Retail costs *Wholesale costs *Multi channel costs *Direct sales costs	* Plan/ strategy * Market penetration * Psychological effects of promotion *Is it cost effective *Who are the early adopters in the segment	*Where to sell service * Distribution channels *Trials *BOGOF * Technology use * Leaflets / posters *Completions/give-away* Direct Marketing * Advertising

Since the introduction of "McCarthy's" 4 p's , some people have argued that its not accurate of is to vague. So and extra Three P's (Booms and Bitners-1981) have been added.
These are shown below.

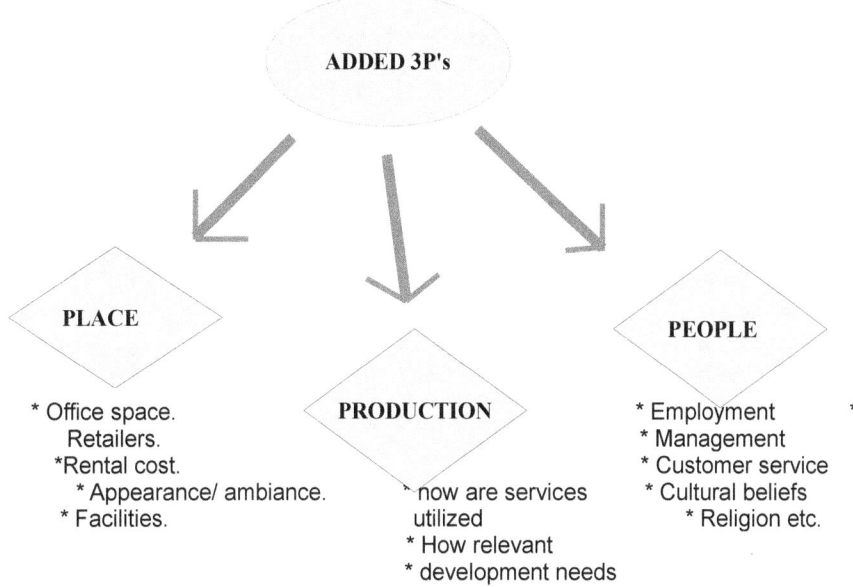

PLACE

* Office space.
Retailers.
*Rental cost.
* Appearance/ ambiance.
* Facilities.

PRODUCTION

* now are services utilized
* How relevant
* development needs

PEOPLE

* Employment *
* Management
* Customer service
* Cultural beliefs
* Religion etc.

SEGMENTS FOR NEW INITIATIVES

When researching and developing new products or services, Ryan-air it need a clear understanding of the segment in which they intend to target. As well as the factors spoken about, the costs, competition etc we need to look deeper into the customer behaviour within the segment. The groups we could use to define such markets could be; demographics, benefits wanted, geographic and psychographic.

If I was to initiate development if a new service of increased winter flights I would concentrate on these aspects to launch the services and grab the attention of the public by defining who your public are. After looking at the differing types of customers I would focus more towards maybe Two of the Four. They would be demographics and benefits sought. Demographics includes things such as, occupation, age, marriage status and disposable income. My reasoning behind focusing on this group is that this includes the two types of customer I would target. Being as Ryan-air are number One in the budget sector I would target youth and business. Students wanting cheap short haul breaks, 18- 30s who look for night-life and not particularly weather, would be I'm sure interested in cheap flight and cheap accommodation due to seasonal pricing.

The business sector, company's send representatives throughout Europe. Ryan-air could target businesses throughout the UK and on the continent in time. The offer discounted flights if they are contracted to your service, I believe would make suitable avenue to test the market in.

Benefits sought- the benefits sought both these consumer groups are similar, meaning a overall promotion strategy, rather than two separate campaigns. Reaching these consumers will be easy, through direct marketing through technology and social media. This avenue of targeting are cost effective with huge scope in regard to the amount of people you can reach.

Both groups are looking for convince, cheap point to point flights, and regular flights to cheaper airports. These services are already well established in the Ryan-air model, therefore selling to these groups would be extremely cost effective leading to bigger profits, and also gaining a larger percentage of the travel market.

If as mentioned briefly the lure of moving into a more broad continental market sounds appealing, a more in depth look into cultural differences, laws, beliefs and religions is needed. They also need to factor in the possible threats such as terrorism, war, or natural disasters depending on the country which they intend to target. The foreign market is more complex to enter for a UK company. Laws may be more restricting, what about employment laws, as they need to employ staff. Employing locals is a good step towards building your brand name and attracting local custom.

SUMMARY

To summarise the information I would say, there is viable markets out there in the travel sector that are ready to exploit. With Ryan-air having a solid and proven model, expanding that to incorporate different markets will fit nicely into there market strategy of keeping cost low. There is no linger the need to spend big on advertising, a little imagination on social media, blogs and forums etc will see the public unknowingly advertise for you through sharing statuses etc. As well ASD boosting winter revenue this will go a long way to rebuilding there already damaged customer perception, meaning longevity.

Understanding The Business Environment

The UK is currently classed as a Mixed Economy, meaning there are two main types og bussiness/ organisation sectors which opereate in our system. These are known as the"Private Sector and the "Public Sector".

The Private Sector is made up of businesses who's main focus or goal is to provide a profit for its members who may include partnerships, Public Limited companys, LTDs or sole traders.

Sole Traders- a business owned by a single person who may have employees

Partnerships- consists a mutually beneficial working relationship between persons who share the responsibilities of that business and the profit gained

Limited Liability Partnership- a rough cross between a Ltd company and a partnership

Not for Profit/ Charitable Organisations- a company that not out to gain personal profit, but to raise finances for relief and research amongst other things.

The Two kinds of organisation I will endeavourer to look into and explain are in my opinion the largest types of organisations.

Public Limited Company (PLC)- to quote a definition used by Andrew Gillespie a Public Limited Company is " A company that is owned by shareholders, but the shares can be sold on the Stock exchange market." Its a company which raises revenue and funding through the sale of shares openly to employees, people looking to invest, basic anyone who wants to purchase them via stock markets such as the FTSE. The majority of people who purchase shares in a PLC are doing so for personal profitable gain, this is ultimately dependant on how a company performs, and wither it is a profitable business. If a company is making a profit or is exceeding its targets, the value of that company's shares will increase, meaning shareholders have the option to sell there purchased share at a profit.

This is where the risk lies, regarding the shareholders of a PLC. If a business fails which you have just bought shares in, the investment made by purchasing the shares will be lost. Research into the market segment which the business operates should be attempted I believe, in order to cut down the risk. If enough is known about the business which you intend to become a shareholder, a good tool to use to weigh up the risk involved is SWOT analysis. Apart from the risk of losing your initial investment, there is effectively no other risks to shareholders in a PLC. They have no legal responsibilities to the company, and are not held accountable for any business debt.

Through selling its Shares publicly a business increases different influences on the company, as there are generally more people who have needs that are expected to be met. Making business decisions becomes more complex, as people from different professional, social, and cultural backgrounds, all with different ideas are looking to have there requirements met, having said that the main objective for all is seen to be financial gain.

Becoming a Public Limited Company is seen by many as the next step up from being a Limited Company, or even for Sole Traders. Its often seen as a method of expansion, of raising revenue for such expansion or to penetrate a different market sector, amongst other reasons for needing a financial injection. On the other hand the perceived downside to this transition is that the Sole trader or the LTD company owner will lose sole power over the business, as selling the shares means more people with a vested interest in your company being financially profitable (see pic1)

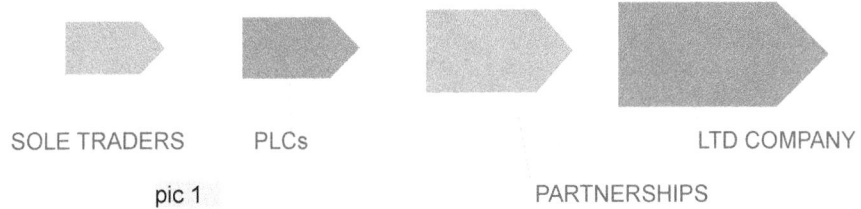

SOLE TRADERS   PLCs   LTD COMPANY

pic 1   PARTNERSHIPS

EXAMPLE OF COMPANY LIFE CYCLE

<u>Private Limited Company</u>- Private Limited Companies or Ltd are also made up of shareholders. These shareholders are usually Employees, Family, Associates or etc. The shares are not floated on the stock market and cant be purchased publicly. The business owner becomes a shareholder on setting up the business.

The Financial risk to shareholders is similar to a PLC and is dependant on the size of the financial investment, they stand to lose their personal investment and are responsible for there own personnel financial issues such as financial assistance from banks The shareholders in a LTD company are more hands on are responsible for certain aspects in relation to the legal factors involved in managing a business. There role is mostly administrative and could include tasks such as being responsible for annual accounts and submitting them and annual returns to company house, in order to remain legal regarding taxes, and contributions.

The other main role in a LTD company is that of the Directors. Its worth sharing that a director doesn't have to be a shareholder and vice versa. The directors are in effect the Mangers of a company and there responsibility is to ensure the company is successful. The Directors have many different tasks in order to achieve this success, and according to the "Company's Act 2006" these include;

- Using skills and experience to aid in the success of a company
- Following company rules
- Making decisions for the benefit of the company
- Communicating any transaction benefits to the shareholders
- Company records and reporting any changes to HMRC and Company house
- Ensuring fair and true company accounts
- Completing self assessment tax returns and registering for self assessment

Its important to point out that many believe the legal and taxation factors in LTD company to be more complex than the previously mentioned Sole Traders, PLC s or Partnerships, and the costs of doing so are likely to higher.

OBJECTIVES, DIFFERENCES AND SIMILARITIES

The objectives or the purpose of a company have many varied factors that may influence the main goal, and each department within a company may have there own personnel objectives in order to achieve the companies overall goal. There are also different categories of objectives which, more so in the current climate are expected to be met, such as legal, and morale objectives.

As the objectives and purposes of business change and evolve over time, the act of defining them becomes more difficult. In order to gain a understanding of such objectives we can split it down using Five main bases (see pic2)

MISSION	A short impact full statement that outlines why a business exists
VALUES	Describes the issues that are of importance to a organisation, a waycapturing public interest
VISION	Sets out what a company aims to be in the future
GOALS	What a company sets out to achieve, where it wants to in future
OBJECTIVES	How it will achieve this goal, what methods will be used pic2

The **Public Sector** consist or businesses and organisations who are controlled by the government and provide a service at a cheaper rate for the good of the general public. Examples of such services are Health care, education, emergency services, and things such as street lighting,and public highway maintenance.

Another side to the public sector are the regulatory organisations who are in place on the whole to offer protection to consumers and businesses alike, organisations such as ACAS, and DEFRA. The objectives of these organisations are not based on providing a profit, but in my opinion there aim is provide stability and longevity of the services for the good of the public and the country.

The public sector although is not a profit seeking sector, the government needs to create a steady source of income in order to keep providing these services. The sources of income can split into Two main groups;

Taxes- This is the main source of government revenue. Its a compulsory payment made by the vast majority of the British public, VAT, working taxes etc. The government aim to use these taxes to cover services such as police, street lighting etc. This means that the tax payer do sent pay for a personnel service but instead pays in to a big pot, which the government decides how and on what services to spend the money.

Non Tax Revenue-This relates to any other other income received by the government. This type of income includes;   a customer pays a fee for a particular service, these fee's are not compulsory and run on the pay if you want the service basis, such services include passport or driving license. these are punishments for people who breach the law or fail to meet certain requirements. Its thought this makes up for just a small portion of the governments income.

These in my opinion are the main avenues of government income. Others include donations, and deficit financing. The objectives differ to a private sector business in the fact that there main goal is not profit driven, but driven to provide a comfortable and stable environment for the general public.

There is a merging line between the Two in some segments of the market, meaning in some occasions the two co-exist and work towards the same targets but for different reasons. There are time were the government will use a private busies to do the work needed for example a council who are building new homes would use a contractor belonging to the private sector. There is also cases were the the Two sectors operate similar services in the same segment for example The NHS and BUPA.

I will take a example of a business from each sector and compare the objectives and endeavour to show any similarities Morrison is a relevant private sector business aiming to build a profit and the NHS is a government controlled organisation offering health care and services through the payment of taxes and money from government distribution.

pic4

MORRISONS PLC → **Mission-** *to provide all customers with the very best value for money on there weekly shop, wherever they live*

Values- *Fresh food, value for money, great service*

Vision- *to be the food specialists for everyone*

Goals- *to be the number one food specialist, to grow from national to nationwide to be in the top times companies to work for*

Objectives- *fresh in-store prep, great selling and service, reduce cost and carbon footprint, great value, and great availability*

THE NHS → **Mission-** *High quality care for all now and for future generations*

Vision- *Everyone has greater control of their health and their well-being, supported to live longer, healthier lives by high quality health and care services that are compassionate, exclusive and always growing*

Values- *Respect and dignity, Improving lives, Commitment to quality care, working together for patients, Compassion, Everyone counts*

Goals- *We create the culture and conditions for theServices staff to deliver the highest standard of care and ensure that valuable public resoursces used effectively to get the best outcome for individuals, communities and society for now and in the future*

Objectives- Prioritize *patients in every decision, listen and learn, inclusive, evidence based, open and transparent, strive for improvement*

As pointed out above , there are many difference between business activity and goals throughout the two main sector. There are also some similarities between the Two but there are not as vast in number compared to the differences.
The Mission for both is to give the best product or service that they can and strive to improve it all the time, leading to the vision which again for both is concerned with growth and improvement that will aid in realising there mission. The values again hold similar meanings and are linked to how they will achieve there vision. The goals and objectives relate to again how they can improve and maintain longevity and continue relaying the service or good to the public, but this is were the differences occur. The both want to meet the needs and wants of the general public,but the reasons for doing this are totally different.
If a private business fails to meet the objective of gaining a profit then it will cease to exist to put it bluntly, however a public organisation doesn't seek such profit, and if revenue is sought it may be gained through the other various avenues touched on previously, e.g. fines or taxes. There is also the option of using a private company as a contractor should any needs arise such as new housing or maintaining the public highways.
There are examples of a public organisation turning to private company methods and floating their shares on the stock market to create revenue, the Post Office being the most recent. Its thought this could be a concern to the public as it could be seen as a way of a public organisation becoming like a private company. In my opinion this is not a good thing as it could lead to increases in prices, due to there aims changing to be more profit related, or the UK economy becoming "Free Economy" which I believe would lead to a lawless, dog eat dog business market.

Stakeholders

Every business regardless of type and ownership has numerous and varying stakeholders, these are those who may or may not have a financial interest or investment but do have a interest in the business or the sector in which it operates. These Stakeholders are from all walks of life and cover a diverse section of people and groups. The stakeholders in a business mean that its not just the financial objectives it need to focus on, objectives sought by the various stakeholders may include legal or morale objectives and social and economical responsibilities. To reiterate this point Edward Freeman pointed out in a speech that value is not only about profit, but covers areas such as;
- Job satisfaction
- Care of the environment
- Less drain on natural resources
- Better value for the community Job satisfaction.

One argument made is that the only objective of a business is to meet the needs of its stakeholders, this in my opinion is almost impossible as there are that many different expectations on a organisation that they cant please everyone. Below is a brief example of the various stakeholders a business seeks to please. (see pic 5)

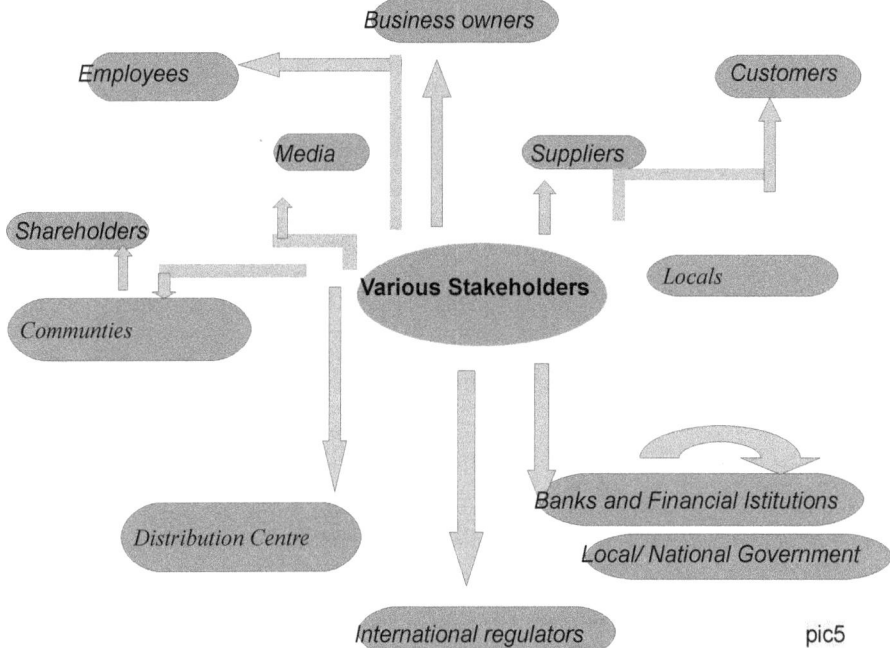

Business owners

Employees

Customers

Media

Suppliers

Shareholders

Various Stakeholders

Locals

Communties

Distribution Centre

Banks and Financial Istitutions

Local/ National Government

International regulators

pic5

As I have tried to show the range of people to please is extremely diverse and difficult to achieve, so the need for stakeholder management is vital. Stakeholder management is the process of identifying the different needs, then prioritising in order of importance and influence, with these most influential groups needs being met first.

There are Four main stages or steps to managing a businesses stakeholders,these are

Identify- identify the stakeholders in a business is the foundation for prioritisation
Analyse- identify/ understand the various influences, there needs, expectations and power
Plan- prioritise by Financial input, power and importance to the company
Engage- communicate strategy to the stakeholders in a developed route

a useful tool to aid in prioritising the influence and importance of the stakeholders is a simple matrix called the Power Influence Matrix, although the simple method can be expanded if needed as shown below. (see pic6)

HIGH	monitor interest and inform occasionally	Keep informed and keep satisfied	key players- engage and keep satisfied
SOMe	monitor interest and keep on side		
LOW	minimum effort	keep informed an explain any changes and reasons	

INTEREST

pic6

POWER AND INFLUENCE

For a company to meet its stakeholders needs they need to take into account other influences from outside the company, issues such as the economy or the environment can influence a company's short term aims. In a poor financial economy the main objective would possibly be to meet the financial needs. Whereas environmental issues may lead to a company to focus on that and building the customers or public perception.

All the issues and sheer numbers of differing groups a business needs to factor into its strategy leads to on many occasions, conflict between various stakeholders, this cant be helped as they may all be pulling in different directions. Examples of such stakeholder conflicts between the groups are common place, the following are common conflicts;

EMPLOYERS VS EMPLOYEES- *when the work force seeks a pay rise or extra benefits BUT the employer seeks to cut cost and streamline the business.*

CUSTOMERS VS SHAREHOLDERS- *expanding the business may be beneficial to customers and employee's and the community through extra choices and higher employment BUT could be seen detrimental to shareholders due to the initial outlay needed*

PUBLIC VS SHAREHOLDERS- *higher profit and dividends is good news for the shareholders investments BUT could have a detrimental knock on effect for the environment due to more manufacturing, distribution leading to increased pollution.*

So after taking all this into account I believe the stakeholders important to Morrison's in this current climate and after there recent poor financial results should be the customers and trying to draw them back into the retail sites. Also the community and certain environmental issue specific to that community will help build up the brand name to where it once was and again increase the numbers passing through there doors on a daily basis. In order to please this category of stakeholders though may cause a conflict with certain financial institute and shareholders who are seeking a quick profit on there investments. The reason for this is for Morrison's to increase customer numbers it will more than likely involve increased spending on a temporary measure through promotions and marketing. So in my opinion the basic Power and Influence matrix for Morrison's would look as follows. (see pic 7)

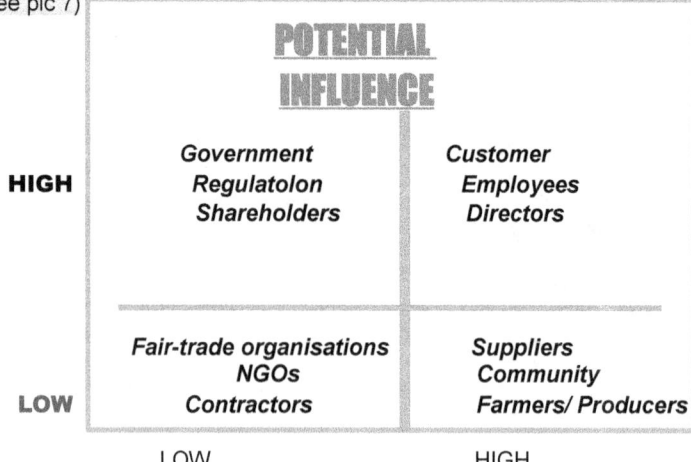

POTENTIAL INFLUENCE

	LOW	HIGH
HIGH	Government Regulatolon Shareholders	Customer Employees Directors
LOW	Fair-trade organisations NGOs Contractors	Suppliers Community Farmers/ Producers

LOW   HIGH   pic7

LEVEL OF INTEREST

This is likely to change or evolve over time as the economy and other external factors change, so stakeholder mapping should be reviewed on a regular basis.

CORPARATE SOCIAL RESPONSIBILTIES

As well as the responsibilities Morrison's have to there shareholders and stakeholders, there are many more responsibilities that need to be factored into their strategy. These are diverse and far reaching as a company in my opinion has a responsibility to all that it comes in contact with and many more that doesn't require contact of any form., these are Morrison's corporate social Responsibilities (CSR).

" A CSR is about how a company manages their business processes to produce a overall positive impact on society." as quoted by Mallon Baker (2007). There are many CSRs Morrison's or any company must adhere to, but on the whole there are covered by Five bases;

Key Business Responsibilities- *to make sure the company is running so that it meets expectations of stakeholders, legal obligations and in a fair way in regard to employees.*

Legal Responsibilities- *following UK and EU legalisations regarding wages,employing foreign workers,following equal opportunity regulations as well as health and safety regulations. There are many more factors to consider.*

Social and Ethical Responsibilities- *focuses on ecological, political cultural factors, how and where goods are produced etc. local communities, packaging, pricing and promotion need to be taken into account here. Although there are rules to follow, I believe if these responsibilities come natural to a business, this will aid in building a brand and longevity.*

Professional Responsibilities- *relates to professional organisations which have rules to follow such as unions. With Morrison's in mind USDAW is a example of a retail union, codes of conduct need to be meet in regards to fair and safe working environments for employees.*

Voluntary Codes- *these are in place to aid in any mitigation or dispute, should be the first step before pursuing the legal avenues. Organisations such as   or the   re examples of voluntary groups*

A companies responsibilities start from the set up, every part of the business needs to be analysed. Form the packaging, materials, distribution methods and location need to be covered.

The same applies to the advertising and marketing campaign, who will see it, different religions and beliefs, and geography are some of the issues here. So as iv e tried to show every stage of a company's process should be looked at regarding its responsibilities. A example I could use is, a product made in China using Ivory and made by under-age cheap labour, would indicate a company is not looking properly at its CSRs, although its cost effective its also morally and legally wrong.

So after this I'm able to further categorize CSRs in to Three broader categories.

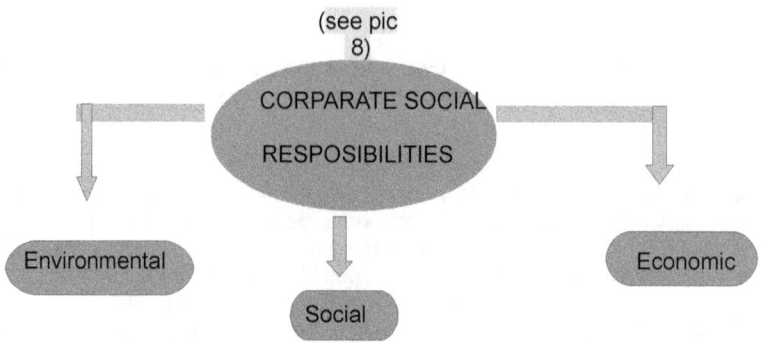
(see pic 8)

CORPARATE SOCIAL RESPOSIBILITIES

Environmental

Social

Economic

Evolving Economies And Their Effects

A Economy is a ever evolving and diverse system which includes factors such as production, distribution and consumption. They are a way of looking at the financial state of a country or area. Economies have been defined in various forms, but it was grundy who said,

" A economy is a evolving pattern of complex human relations, which is concerned with the disposal of scarce resources for the purpose of satisfying various private and public needs for goods and services"

The main factors that a economy needs to factor in to a plan in my are opinion are;

When- *how will the allocation be split between present use and future use*

What *what types of goods and services will be produced*

Who- *who will purchase or use these goods*

How- *how will the goods be produced*

A Economy is vital to the survival and growth of a state, country or in the case of the UK, a group of countries. There are Three types of economy some more successful than others depending on a range of influences. These economies are;

Free Market Economy- *its driven by supply and demand, a economy where everyone is out for them selves*

Command Economy- *this is governed by the government eg levels of manufacturing etc.*

Mixed Economy- *this combines aspects of both, and is the currant economy that is relevant to the UK*

A economy is a fragile system with many influences that may cause a adverse affect on a state and the public and businesses within that state, a poor economy in the said state may then have a knock on effect and cause disruption in another state, and so on. These are known as economic processes. These processes are highly reliant on the successful interaction between various groups within that specific economy. How each group work in harmony or not defines the economic system, examples of such groups are the government, manufacturers, and individuals.

The UK along with the majority of states is now running under a mixed economy, which in theory means both the command and free economies work in harmony for the benefit of everyone within that state. Its not just the economic process that has a bearing on the UK economy. There are many external influences on the UK economy, this is due to import and exports, buying of materials etc. this is a influence to the UK due to the constantly changing monetary exchange rate. If the GBP is weak in comparison with the Euro or the

Dollar this will mean that importing goods will be more costly for the UK, but this in turn is beneficial to the state which we are buying from.. The international integration of economies was once thought of as a good thing, but in recent years some have put the blame there for the downturn in the UK economy and the double dip recession.

With the UK being a mixed economy, our resources are divided between the public and private sectors. The police, defence and fire services are run through the public sector meaning the government, where the private sectors resources are ultimately allocated by supply and demand. IN the UK we do have certain sectors such as healthcare, and post office which are the shared responsibility of both private and public sectors. The success of a economic system is judged by how quickly the state achieves their economy objectives.

When looking into an organisation there are many influential factors the need to be taken in to account. As mentioned the economy and economic system being factors to consider, there are also a vast array of rules, regulations, and legalisations put in place. These rules in a Mixed economy such as the UK are not only set and governed by the government, but through other avenues such as banks and financial institutions and the competition and Markets Authority. There are many more regulatory agencies to be considered her as shown (pic 1).

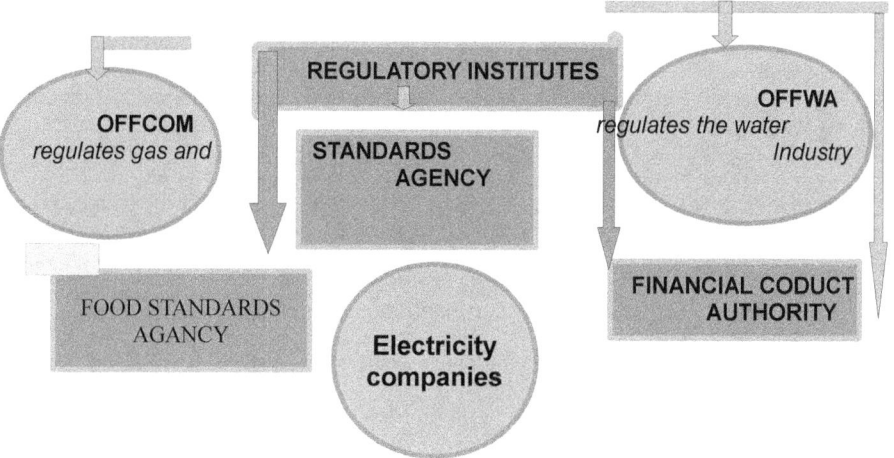

As you can see the majority of regulations are designed to monitor organisations conduct and protect the consumer. One reason for such protection, in my opinion is because of the groups and people who push for the introduction of new regulations. The government and regulators are influenced, lobbied, and some times perused to introduce new regulations, this pressure comes from sources such as

1. Political parties who are seeking the public's backing or vote
2. A government member who is lobbying for change
3. A voluntary organisation
4. Public groups, Public opinion, Public consultancies

so as shown the majority of influences on policies is from groups ran by and are acting in the interest of the general public. The public are not the only influences however, there is also proposals coming from the EU and pressure from many other states. There is vast the amount of different rules and regulation and laws being proposed through the EU, it was reported in the daily mail in 2013 that EU had proposed 3600 new regulations since the general election in 2010.

There are certain acts, policies, regulations and Laws which I believe to be the commandments of businesses, flouting these could result in devastating effects on a company both legally and financially. Such regulations are;

1) The consumer protection regulations covering distance selling, more irrelevant thanks to the internet
2) The consumer protection from unfair trading ergs 2008 covers practices such as aggressive selling
3) Employment law covers how a business treats its employees regarding minimum wage, health and safety and equal opportunity
4) Data protection act there to protect the public data held from being missuses
5) Environmental law this monitors a businesses activity from the start of the process to the end, from production to packaging, distribution to selling.

To form a picture of how these many policies affect UK businesses and the economy, the Budget delivered by the Chancellor of the Exchequer could be seen as a useful tool. Mr George Osbourne starts be reiterating the point that recent crash or downturn in the UK's economy as far reaching and sometimes irreversible effects on everything British. Recession seems to be a circle that is hard to break, less money in the economy means less revenue for UK business, this means less jobs, less disposable income and less spending.

How can we combat or prepare for such a financial crisis? Well carrying on with the Budget speech, George Osbourne touches on the "Fiscal" elements of the economy, and how the government can stimulate the economy. He states that through these Fiscal elements the UK economy is improving all the time, and faster than expected, and is showing the greatest improvements worldwide. This has lead to the budget office reviewing there targets, but he goes onto drive home the fact that a lot more needs to be done to put us back to a strong financial position and stability.

George osbourne predicts through following his methods of fiscal activity could save the taxpayer £1 billion per year. Some of the proposals make good financial sense, others just seem to state the goal without explaining the objectives. A cross section of such proposals looks like this;

1. Manufacture more products in good times to counter act the lean times
2. Cut backs in parliament
3. Decisions to be made to aid in the deficit and protect services such as the NHS and schools
4. Make improvements in the public pension cuts back on the drain on resources in the future

From this yo can see numbers Two and Three offer a idea of what we can do, but no explanation as to how he hopes to achieve this. Aside from certain sections of this budget coming a cross as vague a projecting a image of clutching at straws, on the whole it paints a promising future for the UK economy. As point one above touch on however, with so many influences on the economy via external sources, foreign exchange rates, import and export to unstable states being examples, there is a chance of the same downturn occurring so we need to learn, adapt and be prepared.

As previously stated there are numerous regulations which can lead to legal prosecutions as well as financial crisis to a business. If I look at Retail/ food sector and use Morrison's as a example. The market in which they operate is feircely competitive with new competition emerging frequently. There is certain regulators who monitor this in-case of any foul play or unlawful activity. One of these regulators is the Competitions Market Authority (CMA). To get a picture of the aims of the CMA see (pic 2)

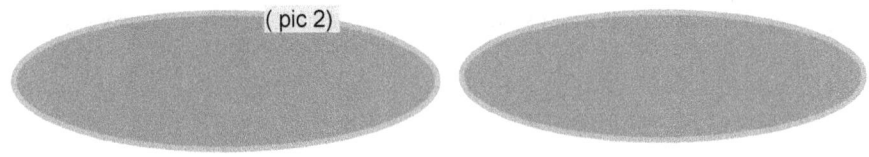

(pic 2)

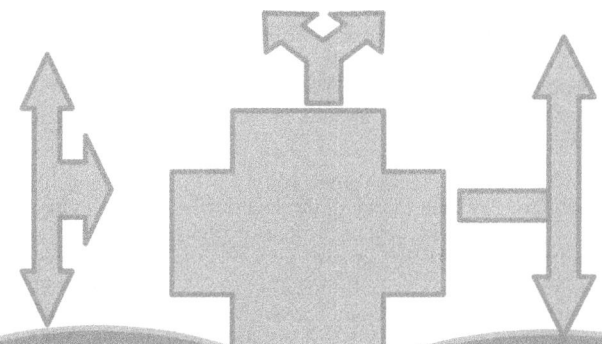

Deliver Effective Enforcement
deter wrong doing, protect consumers and educate businesses

Extend Competition Frontier *to*
aids in the improvement of the way competition works

Refocusing Consumer Protection
promotes compliance and understanding laws and policies

Achieving Personnel Succe
to manage all cases efficiently of the conducting all analysis to the highest standards

Develop Integrated Performance
see that all staff are together in forming fair and effective disciplinary teams

One of the aims of the CMA is to stop what is known as business belonging to "cartels" this involves opposing businesses getting together to fix prices. The reasons could be to create a equal market share, or both agreeing to drive prices up, meaning the customer has no option but to pay the hiked prices. This outlawing of this has aided the customer to get the best value possible if there are willing to research first. Morrison's is in a constant price war with the other leading competition and this leads to the supermarket vying with others to offer the best prices. That is good news for the public as it leads to lower prices and better special promotional offers

Another regulation which of particular interest to Morrison's or so it would seem is the the Employment Law. Since it announced its aim of breaking into the Times best companies, Morrison's seems to be going above and beyond. With the improvement of pension government enforced maybe, they are also aiming to to give their staff the opportunity to gain a QCF professional qualification. Could this be a way to promote their brand, or possibly make *up for* poor employment methods in the past or is it thrust open them, that is open to conjecture.

So it would seem to many that the policies proposed by the government and or other agencies are on the whole in favour of the consumer, and protection them from underhand tactics from the multi faceted companies of today. It would also seem that they are aiding in the recovery and stability of the UK economy, which is at the moment the most important factor financially for this Country. The fact remains however that the number of policy, acts, regulations, legislations and rules is increasing all the time. So the question I leave you with is, where does it end and can it go to far?

THE BUSINESS ENVIROMENT
MARKET FORCES AND ECONOMIES OF SCALE

Market Forces by definition stated in the Collins English Dictionary are " economic factors effecting the price of, demand for , and availability of a commodity." When a organisation is planning to enter a specific market environment its important, regarding success and longevity to take into account the vast and varied factors which could influence the prices, demand, and output of there goods and services.

If we look at a specific environment or sector it may aid in a better understanding of said factors which need to addressed. The food retail sector or the environment in which supermarkets operate is presently fiercely competitive. This environment includes many factors with the potential to to have a positive or negative effect on a business, and its activities, its inputs, and its outputs. Areas such as location, product type, advertising, and pricing amongst others are heavily influenced by these Market Forces, both internally and externally. Examples of external issues faced by a retailer could include, competitors, consumer behaviour, and product variations. Consumer behaviour could be seen as a vague description of a influential factor, as it covers many separate issues such as demographic, geological, and social patterns. The complexity and competitive nature of this market underlines the importance for a business to research and look carefully at the market it intends to target.

To add to the complex issues faced by these organisations, the retail or supermarket environment can be split down into further smaller groups or environments. This is dependant on product variance, different types of consumers, if they plan to market there commodities in the Business to Business market such as cash and carries or plan to go down the more common route for retailers and sell direct to the public. Add to these issues the emergence of the online angle some choose to adopt, and it reiterates the importance of a businesses ability to judge and define there chosen environment. By a organisation getting to grips with these factors, it will aid them in;

- applying better judgement regarding the market size
- providing a more accurate growth forecast
- helps identify any present or maybe future competition
- delivering a market mix which is both relevant and appealing

There are many different models, methods, and aids, which have been introduced over the years to help a organisation better understand there targeted market sector. Models such as S.W.O.T and P.E.S.T.L.E are both useful and relevant examples of such models. *(see fig 1a and 1b)*

S -Strengths	W - Weakness
O - Opportunities	T – Threats

(fig 1a) SWOT shows were the firm is strongest and were it needs to improve. It shows if or where any threat or compositional come from and if the environment shows potential or opportunity for expansion or longevity

P- political	E- economic	S- social	T- technological	L- legal	Environmental

Current political state of the industry	Any prevalent economic factors	How important is culture with in catchment area	Are there any innovations which may help or hinder	Are there any regulations and laws to abide by	Are there any concerns regarding the environment in the industry

(fig 1b) PESTLE tracks a firms chosen operating environment and helps to determine were influential factors may arise from, helping with avoiding them or being better prepared.

These models and methods are not just used as they stand however, there is further scope to split down each aspect in order to show a more detailed focus. One method of achieving this is to adopt the use of " The Five Forces" brought about by Michael Porter *(see fig 2)*

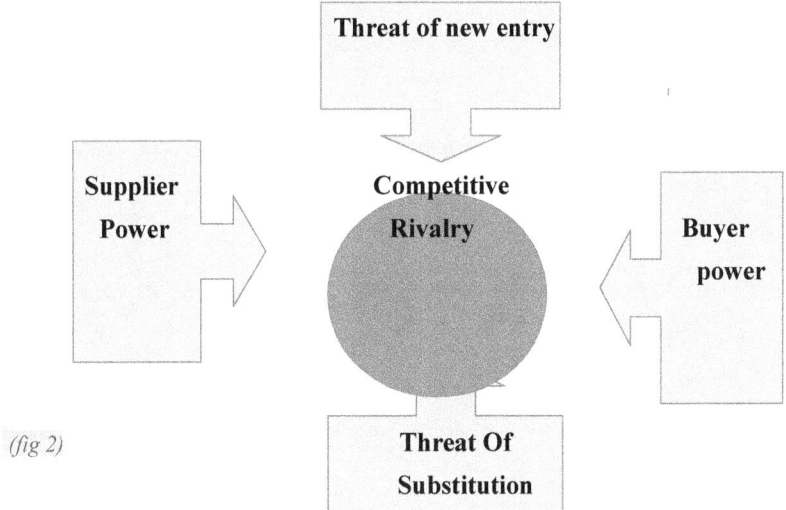

(fig 2)

   This model highlights the factors which influence and put organisations under pressure, it includes cost of entry, costs of materials and how powerful or influential a supplier maybe. The Five Forces takes into account how likely it is that there may be a product similar that may tempt customers away, and the implications of new entrants becoming recognised competition, and if or how the business can adapt.

   The current market environment in which supermarkets operate has changed dramatically over the past decade or so, and it could be said that its undergoing further changes at present. Looking back, retailers consisted of small high-street shops and family run business serving the local community, each having there own catchment area and share of the market. Through this we have seen the emergence of the "Supermarket", large multi national companies who cleverly adapted with consumer lifestyle, offering convenience through there vast range of commodities. The shift in the environment and consumer behaviour at present is changing the environment further. Partly due to tough economic times over previous years, the shift in my opinion has shifted from convince to cost and perceived value. A upshot of this is the emergence of the budget supermarket such as Lidl and Aldi who have entered the market recently and are now challenging the top four chains to be Britons number one food retailer.

   In order to gage where or in what type of market a organisation operates and how that environment may influence there activities, economists came up with a model which sub- divides the retail sector into Four main groups   *(see fig3).*

Characteristics	Perfect competition	Monopolistic competition	Oligopoly	Monopoly
Number of firms	Many	Many	Few	One
Type of product	Identical	Differentiated	Identical or Differentiated	Unique
Ease of market	High	High	Low	Entry Blocked
Examples of industry	Farming	Retail or Restaurants	Making cars or computers	Mail delivery or Gas and Water
Examples of brands	British lion eggs or craven dale	Nan dos or Top man	Ford	Royal mail or Energy suppliers

(fig 3)

This table helps in defining how a market will re-act under different circumstances, it may also be used by start up companies in choosing the correct market to target, the same with companies expanding into further markets.

Looking at the model above, and its relevance to the retail sector can be trying. It could be said that today supermarkets operate within a "Oligopolistic Market." Oligopolistic markets can be categorised or demerited by the following Three main points.

- They consist of a highly concentrated market in which more than One firm dominates.

- The firms set there own prices, independent of government input, but closely linked and mostly in tandem with there competition

- There are certain barriers faced by new entrants who seek to enter the market. A prominent issue would be the high start up costs needed to compete with functioning, successful firms. The different issues a new entrant may face can defined as Natural or Artificial barriers. *(see fig 4a and 4b)*

(fig 4a)

> **Advertising**-- *increased spending from seasoned firms acts as a deter ant*

Predatory pricing-- *a company drops prices to force others out of market*

Limit pricing-- *firms sprices and high output so others fail*

ARTIFICAL BARRIERS

Loyalty *Schemes- help loyal to* seasoned **incumbent** *firms* knowledge of

Superior Knowledge- *a firm may have built vast the market acting as a deter ant*

Exclusive Contracts- *contracts between already existing firms and suppliers foe example makes it difficult for new entrants*

Economies Of Scale- *some firms look to exploit the economise of scale acting as a deter ant*

(fig 4b)

Control of rare materials- costs- *this makes it difficult for compete entrants in relation to competing*

Natural

Barriers

High research and development *for entrants to reach a level to new firms need vast revenue*

High Start up Costs- *a large deter ant including that cant be recalled should yet fail such as advertising*

When relating this information model to the retail sector, its possible to garner information regarding that particular market environment It could be said that the market has many operating firms such as Tesco, Sainsburys, Asda, and Morrisons or collectively known as the top Four. These are the main forces within the retail environment, they is many more vying for a place within the dominant forces such as; Aldi, Lidl , or the CO-OP. All these firms are responsible for there own price strategy, independent of governing body, but when setting prices the supermarkets do so with a eye on the competitions price strategies in order to be able to compete within this busy environment Competition is not the only factor that may effect the prices of goods or services however, they must also take into account economies of scale, the state of the current economy and customer behaviour and there perceived value, and what they are looking for. The reason for the way customers purchase is important, especially within this environment is because the products on sale from the firms, although differ slight through packaging etc they are similar and easily substituted

In order for retailers to maintain or grow there market share, it could said that adopting a "non price strategy" or NPS, is more important than a "competitive strategy", which can be seen as being detrimental for retailers, and will lead to a price war within the environment When setting a non price strategy, some of the factors that can be important to success and can be positively effected by by a business can be seen as; Improving the quality of goods and services as well as the after sales service offered.

- Spending on advertising, sponsorship, or a straggly for effective product placement.
- Promotional activity such as BOGOF or money off promotions
- Loyalty programs now adopted by many retailers

Showing a focus towards a non price strategy is seen by many as wiser avenue to invest in, because it not only has the potential to increase sales, but also the numbers of customer may rise due to customer loyalty and a improved brand name and reputation for offering value. When deciding on which strategy to adopt, organisations may need to look ate the following points;

- What are the chances of the plan working? Has it been tried and tested?
- Is it a plan that can be easily adopted by the competition or copied?
- How high are the costs likely to be to launch the chosen strategy?
- What sort of time scale are they looking at, and is it achievable?

By the organisations adopting a NPS and the concentrated nature of the environment, prices within the market tend to be what is known as "In-elastic, meaning that there isn't a big variance between prices from One firm and another. The UK sees a number of firms spending a large percentage of there budget on offering and advertising special offers, which are likely to change on a weekly basis. The offers tend to be everyday items which most consumers buy, but the firms are trying to catch there eye and draw the customer into making future purchases from them. The main forms of advertising adopted by the main competitors are the like s of TV adverts, websites, blogs or emails, or through the national and local press. Other avenues of promotion used by a lot of retailers includes club cards, seasonal saving clubs, and more prevalent due to the improvement in technology there seems to be more focus on personalised promotions, offering items which you regular purchase via vouchers or emails.

Organisations within a oligopolistic environment make decisions on prices, marketing and advertising factoring many different variances, these can be grouped into Three main groups, making thing s easier to read, and prioritise The three groups are as follows;

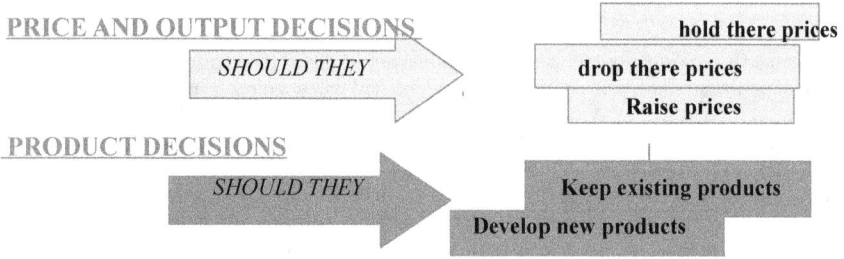

PRICE AND OUTPUT DECISIONS

SHOULD THEY

hold there prices

drop there prices

Raise prices

PRODUCT DECISIONS

SHOULD THEY

Keep existing products

Develop new products

PRODUCT PROMOTION DECISIONS

SHOULD THEY	Decrease advertising budget
	Keep spending constant
	Increase advertising budget

Through detailed research into each group of the decisions that need to be made, organisations are more likely to keep with in budget and time frame, and by doing so are set to reap many advantageous benefits including; greater shareholder profits

- greater market shareholder
- improved survival chances and longevity
- disposal of there competitors.

Having discovered that the retail sector, and in particular Supermarkets lie within a oligopolistic structure. I have also come to the opinion that, there are other other significant quality of other markets that could relate to the Supermarkets. There are certain aspects of the Monopolistic structure that could apply to food retailers. Some of the stand out aspects in my opinion are;

- Many different firms but no one dominates   *this is debatable, but at present there is a slight change in consumer habits thanks to a poor economic state recently, seeing a change from convenience shopping to finding the cheapest option. This has lead to the likes of Aldi and Lidl pushing to be the top retailer.*

- Each have products which differ slightly   *this is the same as in oligopolistic environment, the products are very similar but may differ slight in ways such as packaging, and branding etc.*

- Products on offer can be easily substituted   *again more relevant in today economy and the increased habits of the consumer towards value. It could be seen that if a product is similar and can be found cheaper elsewhere then the consumer is likely to change loyalties.*

The factors which differentiate the oligopolistic and monopolistic market structures are that they are less barriers for new entrants in the oligopolistic structure. The system almost lets organisations come and go as they please it may seem. The knock on effect of this could lead to a new entrant with a different product may yield abnormal profit margins to begin with, largely thanks to customers having limited knowledge of the new product. Over time, as the consumer learns more about the new product, in most cases you would see a fall to normal profit expectations, also partly due to the emergence of substitute products.

The monopolistic market is seen by many to be the most difficult regarding success for organisations, thanks partly to its high competitive nature. As is the case in the oligopolistic market the monopolistic market falls some where between the Perfect competition market and the the monopoly market as shown *(fig 3).*

The monopoly sector consists of one firm, who vends a unique product, with entry for entrants blocked meaning less competition for a firm. This also means less choice for the consumer regarding products and cost, which equals higher profit margins for the organisation. This market seems to have more of a focus on the sale services rather than tangible goods, such as water and gas. The firms have full control of the price structure and its deals on services as they are more necessity rather than a services that is purely desired. Al tough these companies are regulated as seen recently with a government cap on energy price hikes.

The perfect market is truly hard to find, and it could be said that a market that includes, perfect competition, perfect knowledge of the perfect product doesn't really exist. The main characteristics of the perfect competition are:

- High density of organisations but no one really dominates

- The products in many cases are identical

- There is a high volume of buyers who possess excellent product knowledge

- Provides are free to enter environment for new entrants

All these characteristics will lead to a market in which advertising costs are low, as customers product knowledge is very good. Excellent product knowledge may also lead to less competitive outlay as pricing strategies are mostly redundant in this environment. It could be argued that technology has brought us closer to a perfect competition scenario, through the internet making it easier to gain excellent product knowledge.

Examples of organisations operating in this or as close as we can find agricultural, farming and diary companies. These may find that they meet targets because of ease of purchase and distribution, for both vender and buyer.

As found there are many "economies of scale" and "market forces" that will or should influence a business and its activities or a least its decision making process. To be more specific than supermarkets I will be more precise as I try and highlight just some of the the other factors a business should take into consideration.

If we look at fruit and veg for example, a field where there are a massive range of influences on the many firms through out the planning, producing, distribution, and retailing procedure.

Consumers demand for fresh fruit and vegetables has increased in vast numbers over the years, some may say benefiting society as a whole. The reason behind the growth in demand in my opinion is down to the ease in sourcing product information via the internet. It may seem that the companies within this field are pressing home home the benefits of consuming fruit and veg, and with more focus in general on ones physical health, has opened up more opportunities for new entrants, meaning more competition, and as previously stated more competition means more choice and cheaper prices for customers.

Looking from the production side of things, this is not necessarily good news for these companies. With the global market place evolving, showing more consolidations and exclusive contracts between retailers and producers, added to the increase in demand it may seem that the smaller, family run and local businesses are unable to compete on this scale. In my opinion the farming sector, the closest we have to perfect competition is slowly gaining aspects of the oligopolistic market. It would seem that the once price setters, being the farmers are now bit by bit becoming the price takers. It seems the farmers are losing gather bartering power to the dominance of the supermarkets, shown from the low prices offered by supermarkets for commodities sometimes meaning the farmers sell at a loss. With no choice to make these contracts in order to survive, that one big supermarket contract could be worth the large majority of income for these firms.

All this information adds up to the fact that, should a supermarket increase prices to gain larger profit margins, the likelihood is that they will see a fall in sales and demand. Similar or identical produce is all to easy to find, so if the consumer isn't happy with price then they can easily substitute via purchasing the produce from a competitors.

In order to highlight the different factors that effect the commodities that supermarkets deal in I shall chose another product and attempt to show the effecting market forces. Unlike fruit and veg, where a large majority is imported from overseas, there are items stocked on supermarket shelves that don't have to travel as far.

Crisps for example are a product that is produced on British Soil, not only produced however, but the raw ingredients are also produced in house. The means that there are less or different forces at work, the main difference of course is the locality of production takes out a major factor in the importation and the spoilage that may cause. Having said that, there are many other factors that need to figured into the manufactures plans, and that of the retailers. Walkers and KP are both successful crisp manufacturers, there main ingredient being potatoes. The humble potato has a major force that could influence the crop, that is weather. Without the right conditions the farmers who grow the potatoes used by the crisp firms will struggle to reep what they sow. We as humans can not influence the weather so instead the farmers, walkers and the retailers need to factor in a back up plan should the weather cause problems. Having mentioned that the transport issue is greatly reduced, locality is still a influence on the sale of crisp, and the growing of the potato. Within the UK different areas have different soil types,a issue that the farmers must address, before even starting to produce there crops. Different soil conditions may influence the success of there crop and the the price in which they sell to the product manufacturers, which will effect he cost at which the retailers sell to the consumers.

There are many other factors that have a bearing on the cost of crisps, such as;

- Transport- although as stated this influence is not as vast as the imported fruit and vegetables, there are issues which can effect the sales. Price being one as it can some times be cheaper for a country to import rather than produce locally, dependant on the great British weather and how the transport network copes with poor conditions, another could be the cost of fuel and vehicles compared to on the continuant or further a field.

- Buyer Behaviour- As touched on with fruit and vegetables, there seems to be more of a focus on healthy living which could mean a decrease in the sales of items such as crisps, this could mean either price increases for the customer due to less producers, or cheaper prices due to the retailers trying to up the sales of such commodities.

- Location- This effects many other market forces including transport, regarding how far they have to travel, and also the infrastructure meaning the routes and how accessible the routes are. It also effects buyer behaviour, through the type of items customers want. Cities tend to cosiest of fast paced life styles and eat as you go lunch breaks so the crisps stand a good chance here. Rather than country/rural areas where people are more slower in there lifestyle and have more time to eat fresh healthy options

So as we can see although each type of products have different factors to think about, some have more influences than others. This doesn't mean that things get easier, as when One market force is removed from the equation, than another One is added, as seen in transport with crisps. When the travel is removed, the local infrastructure and weather conditions are added to the mix.

From seeing that the demand for a product is dependant on the cost, this tells us that the price is classed as "elastic." Price elasticity of supply or (PES) determines the depth of relationship between the quantity of goods with the price changes. To enable us to see if a supply is elastic or in-elastic there is a formulae which is

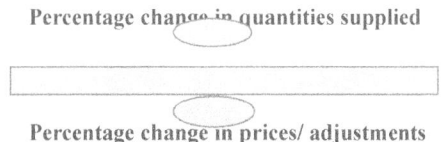

Percentage change in quantities supplied

Percentage change in prices/ adjustments

If the answer to that is higher than 1 the supply is elastic. This is found in the retail of fruit and vegetables. If the answer is lower than one its known as in-elastic, meaning that if a price increases there is only a proportionate change in quantity supplied *(see fig 5a 5b)*

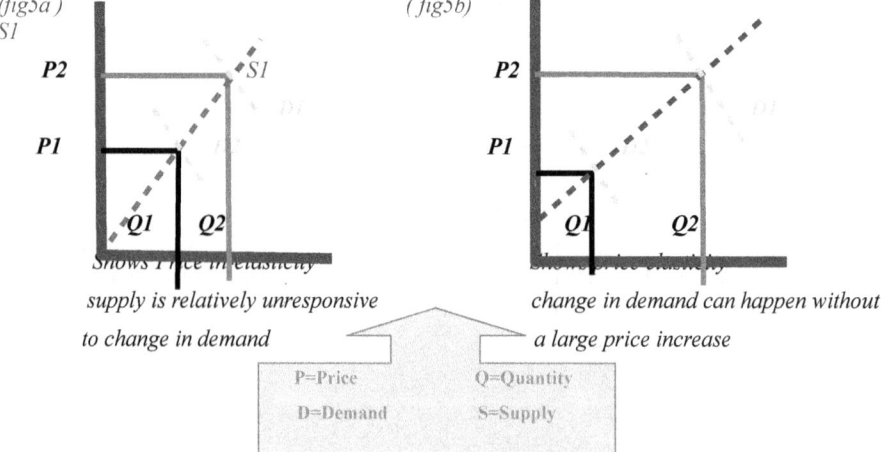

(fig5a)
S1

P2   S1

P1

        Q1   Q2

Shows Price inelasticity
supply is relatively unresponsive
to change in demand

(fig5b)

P2

P1

        Q1   Q2

Shows price elasticity
change in demand can happen without
a large price increase

P=Price   Q=Quantity

D=Demand   S=Supply

Elasticity in supply is dependant on many various factors, including;

- CAPACITY--> does the company or growers have the capacity to grow there output

- STOCK AND MATERIALS--> are the stock/store levels at a level which means a fast response to a change in demand

- FLEXIBILITY--> can a company substitute its adapt its product. Not in the case of farmers, as once a seed is planted then they are tied to a decision for a long period

- PRODUCTION SPEED--> as above difficulties arise in farming as there decisions are made long in advance.

Other factors involved in price, supply and demand are for example; production costs and taking into account the cost of producing extra to meet demand, against revenue gained by selling extra. This is also known as "Marginal costs and Marginal revenues." These can be looked in the Three following ways;

- FIXED COSTS--> show no change as production levels increase or decrease

- VIARABLE COST--> vary in accordance with production levels

- SHOET AND LONG RUN COSTS--> the difference between the two. Short run depending on input may vary long run should be stable.

Distribution is also a major factor regarding supply and cost. As seen over the years distribution methods, and channels have developed and improved massively, making shipping more cost cost effective and efficient. This again adds to a increase in compositional it proves a massive draw to entrants. If we read between the lines, better shipping means produce from exotic destinations. This offers firm the opportunity to market produce that is different from the competition and relatively unknown to some consumers.

The environments nature itself should be delved into by new entrants, before the entry stage. Influential factors here include;

COMPITITION LEVELS

CUSTOMER LOYALTY

AGE OF THE MARKET

COMPANY OBJECTIVES

PRODUCT SUITABLITY

ENTRY/MARKET RESTRICTIONS

An effective method of researching and gathering information on the market in which a company which to enter, the collective factors of influence on price, room for growth and longevity etc can be factored into the SWOT or PESTLE models.

S	W
STRENGTHS	WEAKNESS
O	T
OPPORTUNITY	THREATS

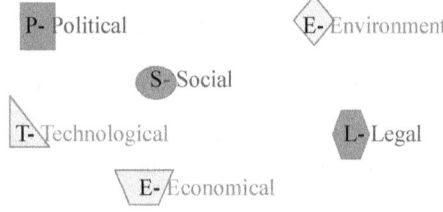

P- Political   E- Environmental

S- Social

T- Technological   L- Legal

E- Economical

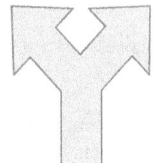

Used in tandem to gain a understanding of customer behaviour, market type, culture amongst many others. SWOT looks at internal and external factors to build a more successful penetration plan

these models can be further researched and looked into using a method which was the brain storm of Michael Porter, called "Porters Five Forces" Which are thought of as;

THREAT OF ENTRY

POWER OF SUPPLIER   COMPETITIVE RIVALRY   BUYER POWER

THREAT OF SUBSTITUTION

This research is vital when monitoring the market and should be undertaken on a regular basis. It will aid in understanding the environment and will assist in spotting opportunities for growth and expansion into other markets. Included in the tasks that if completed regular provide the best chance of survival are internal and external audits included in the SWOT model.

CULTURE FACTORS WITHIN A MARKET

With the growth of multicultural communities within the UK, culture has become more of a influence on the way in which the a organisation may approach a giving market environment. It may also be seen to be a driving force of increased competition within certain environments, as new entrants seek to fill any cultural gaps in the market. Another hurdle faced by organisations is the competition from international markets, as new and already established companies enter the UK market, companies such as Ikea, Lidl, and Aldi.

When talking about culture within a business rather than a environment, its not only factors such as language, beliefs and nationalities, or the external factors that need to be reviewed. The organisation will portray its own corporate culture, which needs to put in place to run along side the external factors. It could said that corporate culture is now more predominant in the strategies of retailers especially. There is or seems to be a focus on how employees and management portray themselves to those who they come in contact with, including social media sites. The culture of a firm is projected through many aspects, including dress codes, business hours, treatment of staff and customers, even aspects such as ambiance plays a part how a company is viewed. A customer both consciously and subconsciously judges every aspect of there experience, and decision are made on culture. Staff behaviour is important as customers seek the whole service from choosing to buying to be hassle free.

The attractiveness of goods and services is all related to perception and how potential customers view them. Many factors of goods and services effect how they are perceived by the customers. The broad spectrum of influences covers both national and international differences. A recent example of such national differences is one concerning a massive brand name. The Sun newspaper was boycotted by the Liverpool FC fans within the city, a direct result of the behaviour of the reporters writing derogatory articles regarding the supposedly poor conduct of fans during the Hillsboro disaster. Although shunned by the majority in Liverpool, it was the best selling tabloid if you travelled just a few miles north.

People who are of different race, religion or creeds, view value in different ways, some seek cheap cost whilst others may seek longevity or a excellent after service. Difference in the consumers habits are down to various reasons

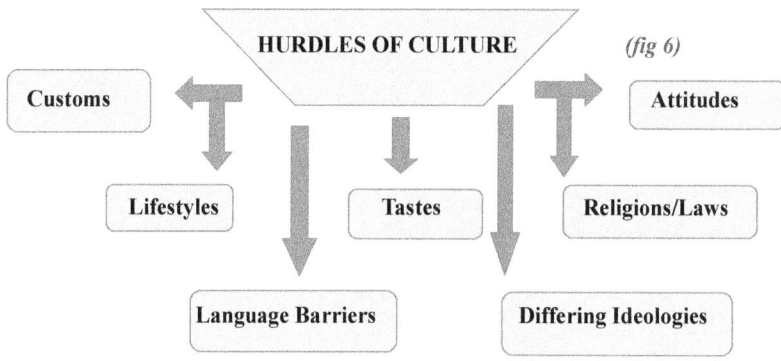

If we look at the various hurdles there are many aspects of the community which they serve which are of importance when choosing your strategy

Language--- Different languages use some word which sound the same but have different meanings, this is important regarding packaging and advertising. Theses difference even occur between nations that speak the same language for example the UK and the USA. Chips and gas are examples of the same words with different meanings.

Lifestyle--- Lifestyle is another big factor, in the cities buyer behaviour differs to the more suburban or rural areas. City life tends to lend itself to a fast paced lifestyle consisting of fast food, eat as you go purchases, where as in rural are s lifestyle may be more planned and careful purchasing, I believe that disposable income and price of living also plays a part in this.

Tastes--- Tastes differ not just geographically but person to person. The upshot being that its impossible to please everyone. Range could be seen to be the answer to this, as we supermarkets investing in more exotic ranges to meet the demand of the growing multi cultural societies.

A good tool to understanding cultural differences in a contrasting way is the "Emic and Etic" method, a phrase coined by linguist Kenneth Price. Etic is the view from the outside where as emic is the view of culture within a business or environment.

A quote from Ager and Loughry in 2004, concerning human nature in regards to the social system said,

"Etic knowledge refers to the generalisation about human behaviour that are considered universally true and commonly links cultural procedures to factors of interest to the researcher such as economic or geological conditions, the culture insiders mat not consider to be relevant"

To define Emic behaviour I will take a quote coined by Morris in 1999.

"Emic knowledge and interpretations are those existing within a culture that are determined by local or custom, meaning and beliefs." To show what this means to a business environment a simple illustration is used to simplify the process. *(see fig7)*

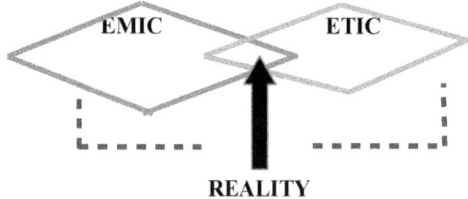

When looking in to the insider and outsiders perspective or etic and emic we should keep in mind the following;

EMIC

- it considers attitudes and interests that are unique in a giving culture

- emphasis is on the context of each country and understanding its culture

- relating to similarities and differences internationally which could be see to be judgemental

ETIC

- _identifies and assess universal attitudes and behaviour and a focus on the development of a cultural free market

- knowing that businesses look to find similarities across markets not differences

- knowing similarities mean opportunities for the transfer of activities or strategies across different markets

Integration or universal marketing is becoming more common thanks to globalisation, this is of benefit to businesses, as outlay decreases due to more cost efficient marketing and research options, and development to penetrate a foreign market. Reasons for this is open to interpretation, one could be seen to be that globally, goods and services demanded are becoming identical. To show this look at McDonald Fast food, there products are the same worldwide, because consumers today no matter where they reside have access to the same movies, music, and holidays for example. This is a contributing force driving globalisation.

When understanding cross cultural business dealings, it was thought best by Richard Harris to decipher the trading countries in to Three groups.

- **MULTI ACTIVE**--- these counties tend to display there feelings openly with emotive confrontation, they often interrupt but with good reasons. They are impatient and can be often seen to adapt the truth. They wear there heart on there slave and often put feelings before fact and these attributes often spread into social aspects of the country. Included in this are countries such as;

- **LINEAR ACTIVE**---these tend t be respectful of authority and be polite whilst being direct. They listen as well as talk and early interrupt. They opt for truth over diplomacy and confront problems with logic. Included in this are countries such as;

- **REACTIVE**--- these tend to listen a lot of the time and hide there feelings , rarely causing confrontation, they are very polite and never interrupt, they are people orientated and keep promises, they opt for diplomacy over fact. Included in this are countries such as;

To to summarise, its plain to see that there are many factors, market forces and economies of scale, which effect every stage of a businesses activities. From planning to development and packaging, from distribution to retail and after sales The price, the product, and conduct of a organisation are largely dependant on culture, with culture covering a diverse group of factors. Such factors should be reviewed on a regular basis in order to strive to achieve longevity with a favourable profit margin.

GLOBAL FACTORS INFLUENCING BUSINESS ACTIVITY

International trading is a large and vital form of revenue for the UK or any state that equipped with the infrastructure and a source of materials to manufacture and distribute goods and service s It would seem from reading g the Office of National Statistics (ONS) published data, that after a poor period of low exports and financial crisis, that trade stars for the UK are once again looking positive.

The ONS paint a glowing picture of the present and growing state of output for the Uk's exports, with statistics pointing to a swift growth. The figures published so that the UK is presently trading at;

⏱ **+91% ON DEALS WITH CHINA**

⏱ **+118% ON DEALS WITH RUSSIA**

⏱ **+57% ON DEALS WITH SOUTH KOREA**

These seem to be very healthy figures, and if the new targets are to be met than the future of the UK economy on the international front looks good. Amongst the targets set by the UK are;

⏱ **a 100,000/ 25% increase on UK firms trading internationally**

⏱ **expand international activity across Asia, and South America**

So what has changed in order for the Uk's export and international trade to show healthy figures? Over the last few decades international trade on a whole has seen a vast growth, One reason for that in my opinion is down to globalisation, amongst many contributing factors for the growth. The world economy is now Eight times bigger than it was in 1950, the reasons behind this a vast but the things that stand out to me are the following;

TECHNOLOGY--- On the whole technology has been seen to improve most aspects of business, making things easier and more cost effective. Financial transactions are now pretty much instant and at a press of a button, communication is made easier and in most cases free, and distribution is more quicker and cheaper.

DISTRIBUTION--- Faster transport via air, faster rail links and the ability to source materials or goods from anywhere in the world is a big factor, meaning cheap and effective distribution. In some cases it may make more financial sense to import a material rather than produce it internally.

DEALS BETWEEN STATES--- Comparative advantage dee's Two countries who export similar goods to come together in a beneficial deal for the both of them. If both states deals in TV and also Cars for instance. They look at the figures to see who it would make more sense to focus on One of the products, whilst the other state concentrates on the other. This enables both to reap health market shares and have a steady stream of trade with the partner state.

The question is, how if the world economy is predicted to slow in its growth, why are the UK setting such high targets? Is it because its membership in the European Union (EU)?

There are many arguments for and against the UK's involvement in the EU. There are also many like myself who are undecided. The EU certainly opens up new opportunities for new trade and to build on existing contracts. Opportunities such as comparative advantage with other member states. Deals with other members regarding raw materials or expansion within that country may also be a possibility. The introduction of the Euro , a single multi nation currency is a debate with many strong and vocal arguments. One advantage is of course, the reduce of the risks involved in international trade posed by inflation rates. This argument could also used against a single currency, because if the UK trade and economy is set to grow then we risk the chance that we will lose out on the pound being a leader in the currency market. There is also the advantage of financial bale outs or help if needed.

Other aspects in favour of trade growth in the UK could;

>> The UK has a vast and multi cultural society, including many different nationalities, beliefs and cultures. This could be seen to increase trade and boost the economy on the grounds that it is creating closer integrated economies both socially and business wise. More businesses in the address book mean more opportunities, that is understood in any country you may be contemplating entering.

>> Technology is leading to better information and quicker and more efficient learning. This is leading to today's generation learning important skills a generations faster. A upshot of this is that there are more markets in the world economy, and increased output from new emerging or improving states. Benefits of this are more trading opportunities with new states offering new products. It may also open up more efficient distribution routes by decreasing cross border regulations or any past hostilities.

>> Moving the resources and skills to be more cost efficient is seen as both a advantage and a dis-advantage. Its good in the fact that we can distribute skills and knowledge through personnel, this aids production costs as moving to certain countries has benefits. Moving to a production operation to China cuts labour and resourcing cost through its cheap labour market, or a Bookmaker moving to Gibraltar to cut back on the taxes that they pay makes sound business sense. It also aids our economy in the same way as we attract the highest qualified professionals from abroad, thus strengthening services and trade. The downside however is that the bodies which cross the channel are not all here to aid in economic growth. This is putting a strain on the benefit system as well as Education, Police and NHS. Another argument is that it cause higher unemployment for workers originating from the UK

Global advantages of a integrated market, quicker learning and distribution of skills is the decline of the G7 or developing nations and the increasing size of the group known as the BRIC economies. Developing or G7 countries are those who have little household income disposable or otherwise, with little trade output. They have previously been exploited by foreign companies seeking cheap materials or workforce. This is slowly changing a she economies grow meaning better income, better education and improved global trade. These states may then be considered to enter the BRIC category. This includes states with improved or improving standards of infrastructure, political stability and living / working conditions. The phrase BRIC states was a brain child of Jim O Neil of Goldman Sachs, used to describe Brazil, Russia, India, and China, who were at the time in period of transition. The list of BRIC states has now come to include;

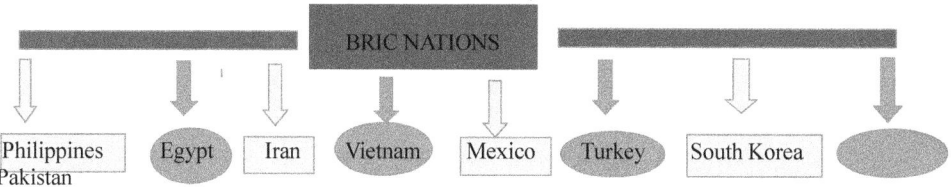

Although the emergence of new economies offers opportunities, the UK has many issues to address before negotiating. The unique differences between nations, different audience and perceived value and different cultures are potential banana skins for entrants into a new states economy.

Globalisation, a good thing or a bad thing? It seems opinion is still split, but I belie a lot of good has come as a result, although most points are open to interpretation and many aspects still provoke strong opinion such as the formed coalitions like the EU.

With all the trade within the the EU and BRIC communities, there must be some form of governance, with any country or businesses entering a trade route with another rules must be set in place an known by both parties. The areas that need to be regulated are very large in number, covering things from Fair trade to protectionism and all that lies between. The free market sets no rules as trade between nations regarding the flow of goods and services, some of the benefits can be seen below *(see fig 8)*

More choice- manufactures have cheaper sources of

materials meaning cheaper prices

It promotes free and fair inflation

competition and encourages

entrepreneurs

FREE

TRADE

BENIFITS

less pressure regarding

as prices are set low

promotes economic growth through increased

input and outputs

(fig 8)

The are risks associated with trading internally, even within the EU, mostly due to the many deals and trade happening all the time. The EU for example consists of 28 nations who are all linked through membership, as as well as trade and other legally bound interactions. This has seen the emergence of many and varied regulating bodies. Some of the regulators that govern the international trade environment include;

WORLD TRADE ORGANISATION-- This organisation was set up in 1995, it took over the role once held by the "General Agreement on Tariffs and Trade (GATT). They are responsible for monitoring trade between nations and seeing that the trade rules are adhered to.

FAIRTRADE AGREEMENT (FTA)-- This is more of a agreement or contract, rather than a regulating body. Its seen as a legally bound commitment between Two or more countries or states. The objective of this particular agreement is to liberalise the access to each others good or services. It is also likely to include agreements on government procedures, competition policy, and property rights.

Regarding the UK and FTA, the UK is unable to negotiate any of its own fair trade agreements due to its membership in the EU. Having said that they are party to over Fifty fair trade agreements in which the EU is prescribed to.

__FAIRTRADE ZONES--__ This term as a wide range of issue to factor in to its activities. Its used to describe the agreement entered by members of a specific bloc in order to promote trade between the Bloc's members.

In the USA its known as the   . It relates to the rules regarding the landing, handling, manufacturing or adjustment of a product without intervention from customs imposed taxes. The involved organisations are only subject to such taxes once the commodity is past on to the consumers.

Another major regulation is that of the EU's competition policy. Especially within the oligopolistic market businesses are under pressure to offer the best quality goods are the lowest prices. This is due to the threat of substitution. A outcome of this is that firms may try to limit there competition by;

making agreements with there rivals known as cartels, they make there own rules to cut the competitive edge.

they may abuse there dominance and try to squeeze there rivals out of the market.

mergers where the rival firms join forces to share market dominance.

The competition policy is there to protect the consumer as well as other firms. By governing this rule they make sure thee is healthy competition within the market and of course this means lowers prices to the customers as the firms try to out sell each other. It also contributes to greater choice, as the firms try to be innovative in order to maintain longevity. A positive from a business point of view maybe that because of the sustain competition within the EU, there are more capable of holding there own in the other markets worldwide. In order to maintain the policy the EU looks further than the company itself, they also take into account the sourcing of materials, manufacturing the products and the distribution methods. So it may be said that this policy covers most aspects of a businesses activities within the EU.

So with many Global factors influencing the many aspects of trade between various nations, the environment is highly complex, possibly to complex for some firms to attempt to enter this market. There are many advantages to international trade including cheaper materials and production, deals between nations with a positive output, and partnerships are mostly more cost efficient On the flip side they are high volume of risk involved some of which may be fatal for some organisation. This is why the proper research in to all aspects of the market are vitally important. Research and looking g at5 it in a detailed way is not the only aspect that leads to success. The role played by the regulators, governments and financial institutions is one of importance. They are there to protect not only the trading organisation, but the countries economy as well as the consumers.

www.ingramcontent.com/pod-product-compliance
Lightning Source LLC
Chambersburg PA
CBHW070744180526
45168CB00004B/1528